3 0000 005 900 018
LIBRARY OF MICHIGAN

D1299463

MICHIGAN STATE UNIVERSITY

On the Banks of the Red Cedar

EDITED BY LARRY BIELAT

COURAGE
BOOKS

AN IMPRINT OF RUNNING PRESS
PHILADELPHIA • LONDON

To all the men and women who have made Michigan State the great university it is today.

And to those coming after who will add to its glory.

© 1998 by All Sports Art and Publications, Inc.

All rights reserved under the Pan-American and International Copyright Conventions

Printed in the United States

This book may not be reproduced in whole or in part, in any form or by any means, electronic or mechanical, including photocopying, recording, or by any information storage and retrieval system now known or hereafter invented, without written permission from the publisher.

9 8 7 6 5 4 3 2 1
Digit on the right indicates the number of this printing

Library of Congress Cataloging-in-Publication Number
98-71221

ISBN 0-7624-0492-2
Marching Band Edition 0-7624-0493-0

PUBLISHED BY COURAGE BOOKS, AN IMPRINT OF
RUNNING PRESS BOOK PUBLISHERS
125 SOUTH TWENTY-SECOND STREET
PHILADELPHIA, PENNSYLVANIA 19103-4399

Mich
LD
3248
.M5
B53
1998
c.2

"Beaumont Tower stands

as a symbol of the

will and ideals

of the men who brought

higher education

to the common man."

PATRONS

MSU
BOOKSTORE
INTERNATIONAL CENTER
(800) 242-6620

DOWNTOWN COACHES
OFFICIAL SUPPORT GROUP OF
SPARTAN FOOTBALL SINCE 1946

MSU REBOUNDERS
OFFICIAL SUPPORT GROUP OF
MSU BASKETBALL

MSU BLUELINE CLUB
WORLD'S LARGEST HOCKEY
BOOSTER CLUB

JUDY AND DUANE VERNON
*"MSU has done more for us
than we can do for MSU."*

DICK AND DOLORES
WHITE
COLDWATER, MICHIGAN

DAVE CARRIGAN
KALAMAZOO, MICHIGAN

JAY LOUWERS

TOM SEARL

JIM ADAMS

the College Store
4790 SOUTH HAGADORN
WWW.THECOLLEGESTORE.COM

ALL SPORTS ART & PUB.
INC.

MICHIGAN STATE UNIVERSITY ALUMNI ASSOCIATION

SMITH BARNEY
A MEMBER OF TRAVELERS GROUP

STUDENT BOOK STORE
"Go State, Go SBS!"

SEARS
FRANDOR
"Come see the Spartan side of Sears."

Citizens
Bank
Citizens Banking Corporation
17 LOCATIONS TO SERVE THE
MSU COMMUNITY

RENO'S EAST SIDE
HOME OF THE RON MASON SHOW

WOHLERT
CORPORATION

JIM CHIDESTER
JBC TREE FARM

CENTURYTEL
KEEPING SPARTANS CONNECTED

SANDY WALTER AND
ASSOCIATES INC.

LARRY MARTIN
OVID ELSIE, MICHIGAN

MARTY COATES AND
JERRY MARSHALL
"Privileged to be the 'Voice of the Spartans.'"

VINCE AKSAMIT

History In 1855 the State of Michigan purchased 677 acres of land at $15.00 each from Colonel A. R. Burr to build a college to teach agriculture. The property 3½ miles east of the capital was flanked by a dirt road from Detroit (Grand River Avenue) on the north and the Red Cedar River on the south, Harrison Road on the west and Bogue Street on the east. There are walks, drives, rustic bridges, lawns, flower borders, and groves in pleasing variety throughout the campus along with the buildings in a park environment.

The Capital Building
for the State of Michigan

The steps of the capital were often used for campus
celebrations, as shown here in 1912—after the
35–20 football victory over Ohio State.

In 1925 Michigan Agricultural College (MAC) became Michigan State College (MSC). The initials still overlook the campus from the now abandoned Power Plant smoke stack next to Spartan Stadium.

In 1955 MSC became Michigan State University. The main campus (2,100 acres) is often referred to as the most beautiful in the world. In the early 1900s, visitors came from great distances to spend the day at "College Park." Today more than 3,000 additional acres are devoted to experimental farms and natural areas. The university has fourteen degree-granting colleges for more than forty thousand students who come to East Lansing from 113 nations. Eighty overseas programs exist in thirty countries. Michigan State as of 1997 has produced sixteen Rhodes Scholars.

F.I. Lankey

the MAC yell leader, wrote the first version of the Fight Song as he returned from a 12–7 football victory over Western Conference Champion Wisconsin in 1913. Lankey, a WWI Air Force Lieutenant, died a few years later, in 1919, in a plane crash.

THE ORIGINAL FIGHT SONG

ON THE BANKS OF THE RED CEDAR
THERE'S A COLLEGE KNOWN TO ALL;
THEIR SPECIALTY IS FARMING,
BUT THE FARMERS PLAY FOOTBALL.

AGGIE TEAMS ARE NEVER BEATEN,
ALL THRU THE GAME THEY FIGHT,
FIGHTING FOR THE ONLY COLORS,
GREEN AND WHITE.

SMASH RIGHT THRU THAT LINE OF BLUE,
WATCH THAT SCORE KEEP GROWING,
AGGIE TEAMS ARE SURE TO WIN,
THEY'RE FIGHTING WITH A VIM.
RAH! RAH! RAH!

MICHIGAN IS WEAKENING,
WE'RE GOING TO WIN THIS GAME;
FIGHT! FIGHT! RAH, TEAM, FIGHT!
VICTORY FOR M.A.C.

The MSU Fight Song adopted new words in the 1970s.

SPARTAN FIGHT SONG

ON THE BANKS OF THE RED CEDAR
IS A SCHOOL THAT'S KNOWN TO ALL;
IT'S SPECIALTY IS WINNING,
AND THE SPARTANS PLAY GOOD BALL;
SPARTAN TEAMS ARE NEVER BEATEN,
ALL THROUGH THE GAME THEY FIGHT;
FIGHT FOR THE ONLY COLORS,
GREEN AND WHITE.

GO RIGHT THRU' FOR MSU,
WATCH THE POINTS KEEP GROWING.
SPARTAN TEAMS ARE BOUND TO WIN,
THEY'RE FIGHTING WITH A VIM.
RAH! RAH! RAH!
SEE THEIR TEAM IS WEAKENING,
WE'RE GOING TO WIN THIS GAME.
FIGHT! FIGHT! RAH, TEAM, FIGHT!
VICTORY FOR M.S.U.

Union Building

Originally referred to as the Union Memorial Building to honor alumni who died in WWI. The cornerstone was laid in June 1924. The building was sufficiently completed to accommodate the sophomore prom and alumni reunion in June 1925. Built close to the city of East Lansing at the boulevard (Abbott Road) entrance to the campus, it linked "town and gown."

THE UNION BUILDING PROJECT RAN INTO FINANCIAL PROBLEMS FROM THE START. "EXCAVATION WEEK" IN NOVEMBER OF 1923 WAS ORGANIZED BY ALUMNI DIRECTOR ROBERT J. MCCARTHY TO HELP DEFRAY COSTS. STUDENTS AND FACULTY WORKED HALF DAYS DIGGING THE BASEMENT (TOP) WHILE COEDS SERVED DOUGHNUTS AND COFFEE AND THE SWARTZ CREEK BAND (ABOVE) PROVIDED ENTERTAINMENT.

GILCHRIST DORM, PART OF THE LANDON, YAKELEY, WILLIAMS, MAYO, AND CAMPBELL COMPLEX OF TUDOR-STYLE DORMS REMINISCENT OF ENGLISH COUNTRY HOMES. EACH DORM WAS NAMED FOR A WOMAN WHO MADE A CONTRIBUTION TO EARLY MAC. ON THE NORTHWEST SIDE IS A GROVE OF TREES AND A STONE MARKER DEDICATED TO MAC STUDENTS WHO GAVE THEIR LIVES IN WWI.

Alice B. Cowles House

University President's Home. Used for many university receptions and other social functions, it is the oldest building on campus, built on Faculty Row with bricks made from clay from the Red Cedar. Funds from the Fred C. Jenison Estate were used to renovate this brick "farm cottage" in 1941, when its name was changed to honor Jenison's mother. The house is listed on the state register of historic sites.

MICHIGAN STATE UNIVERSITY
PRESIDENT PETER MCPHERSON
AND FIRST LADY, JOANNE.

THE RED BRICK FARM HAD MANY USES BEFORE
BECOMING THE PRESIDENT'S HOME IN 1941.

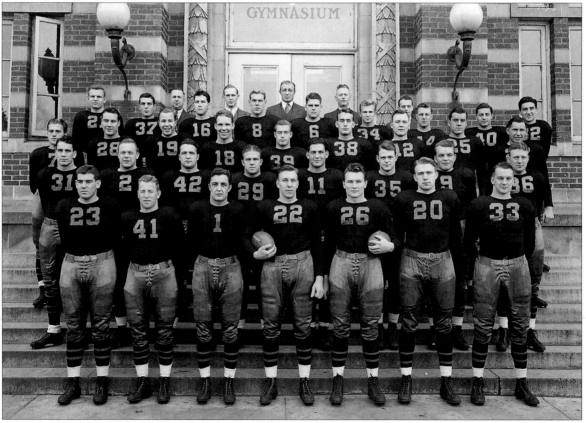

(TOP) I. M. CIRCLE, FORMERLY WOMEN'S GYM.

(BOTTOM) THE STEPS WERE ALWAYS USED FOR "AGGIE" TEAM PHOTOS.

School of Music and Practice Building—
tailgaters' paradise. In 1907, 20,000 people gathered on this field to hear President Theodore Roosevelt speak. The seniors for the first time sang the university's original Alma Mater: "Close beside the winding Cedar's sloping banks of green, spreads thy campus, alma mater, fairest ever seen."

William James Beal, *Botany Professor at MAC in late 1800s. Dr. Beal is credited with much of the early research and development of hybrid corn.*

BEAL BOTANICAL GARDEN

IN 1873, DR. BEAL AND STUDENTS BEGAN A GRASS GARDEN ON THIS SITE NOW NEXT TO THE LIBRARY. IT IS THE OLDEST CONTINUOUSLY OPERATED TEACHING FACILITY OF THIS TYPE IN THE NATION. MORE THAN FIVE THOUSAND PLANT SPECIES ARE LABELED FOR STUDENTS AND VISITORS. THE RUSTIC SETTING INCLUDES A POND, WINDING PATHS, AND THE NEARBY RED CEDAR.

Museum, once the College Library, stands in the center of campus next to Beaumont Tower.

THE RELIEF ON THE NORTH SIDE
SHOWS THE SOWER, WITH THE INSCRIPTION,
"SO AS A MAN SOWETH, SO SHALL HE REAP."
THE MONUMENT RECALLS ENGLISH
CHURCH TOWERS, WITH ONE
SPIRE EXTENDING TO A GREATER
HEIGHT THAN THE OTHERS.

Beaumont Tower

built in 1928 on the original site of Old College Hall.
Old College Hall was the first structure in the world built
expressly for the teaching of scientific agriculture. The site
pictured here was referred to as the "sacred space." The
104-foot tower, donated by the Beaumont family, houses a
forty-seven-bell carillon, each bell weighing from twenty
pounds to two tons (total 120,600 pounds), presented to
MSC in 1929. The tower was named for John W.
Beaumont, a Detroit lawyer who graduated from MAC in
1882. The bells and clock were renovated in 1991.

Agricultural Hall,

built in 1909 at a cost of $182,000, was the finest building on campus at the time. Farm Mechanics, Animal Husbandry, Agronomy, and Soil Chemistry were some of the subjects taught in this building.

Linton Hall was built to house the library and museum. It is the second-oldest building on campus, constructed in 1881, and faces the "sacred space." It later became the Administration Building and now is home to the Graduate School and the College of Arts and Letters.

THE STONE DRINKING FOUNTAIN—OFFERING WATER FOR HORSES ON ONE SIDE, PEOPLE ON THE OTHER—WAS A GIFT TO THE COLLEGE BY THE CLASS OF 1900.

(TOP) EUSTACE HALL, BUILT IN 1888

(ABOVE) MARSHALL HALL, BUILT IN 1902

Laboratory Row

(TOP) OLD BOTANY, 1892

(ABOVE, LEFT) CHITTENDEN HALL, 1900

(ABOVE, RIGHT) COOK HALL, 1889.

MORRILL HALL

BUILT IN 1900 FOR THE PURPOSE OF HOUSING AND EDUCATING
WOMEN, IT WAS NAMED FOR JUSTIN S. MORRILL, WHO
AUTHORED THE LAND GRANT ACT SIGNED BY PRESIDENT
ABRAHAM LINCOLN IN 1862, WHICH LED TO MICHIGAN STATE
BECOMING THE FIRST LAND-GRANT UNIVERSITY.

HUMAN ECOLOGY

FOUNDED IN 1896, IT IS THE THIRD-OLDEST COLLEGE ON CAMPUS.
ORIGINALLY NAMED HOME ECONOMICS.

Libraries MSU's main library and thirteen branches around the campus together house a
collection of more than four million volumes. The special collections division contains
more than 250,000 volumes, including the rare book collection. A unique feature of the collection is the Voice
Library—more than fifty thousand recordings of every major personality of the twentieth century—donated in 1961
by G. Robert Vincent, who worked for Thomas Edison and was the chief sound engineer at the Nuremberg Trials.

THE FOUNTAIN IN FRONT OF THE LIBRARY WAS A SENIOR-CLASS GIFT.

STUDENTS BURN THE MIDNIGHT OIL AS FINAL EXAMS DRAW NEAR.

N A. HANNAH ADMINISTRATION BUILDING

JOHN A. HANNAH ADMINISTRATION BUILDING

NAMED FOR FORMER MSU PRESIDENT JOHN HANNAH (TOP, RIGHT),
WHO SERVED FROM 1941 TO 1969 AND WAS RESPONSIBLE FOR
THE GREATEST PERIOD OF GROWTH IN MSU HISTORY.

Behind the Administration Building,
a favorite spot for students and visitors.

Auditorium

Built in 1940, it has served many purposes. The MSC Lecture Concert Series was one of the best in the nation. Eleanor Roosevelt, wife of the United States President, addressed 5,300 here in March that first year. Dances, banquets, registration, conferences, and exhibits all have been held in this spacious building.

George T. Fairchild Theater

Included on the east side of the Auditorium is an intimate stage named for the inspirational professor of English who went on to become President of Kansas State University.

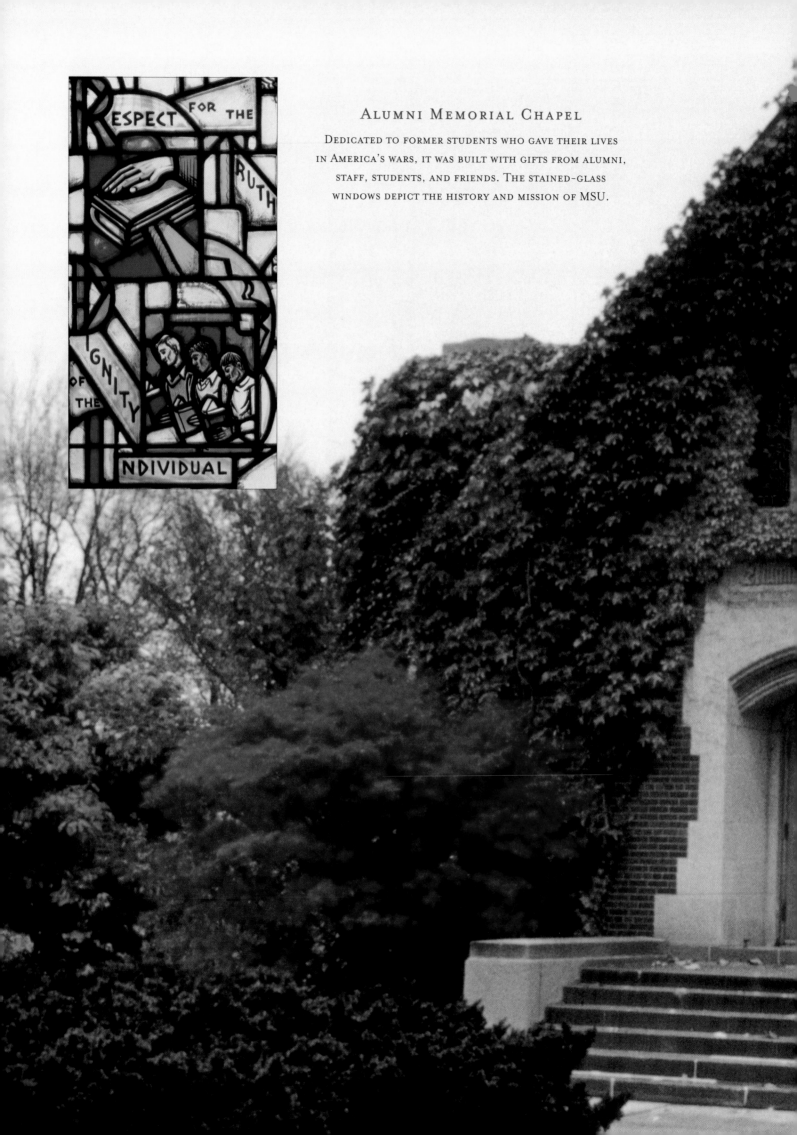

ALUMNI MEMORIAL CHAPEL

Dedicated to former students who gave their lives in America's wars, it was built with gifts from alumni, staff, students, and friends. The stained-glass windows depict the history and mission of MSU.

Business College Complex—Eugene C. Eppley Center and the new Business Building. Located in this complex is the Eli Broad College of Business and the Eli Broad Graduate School of Management.

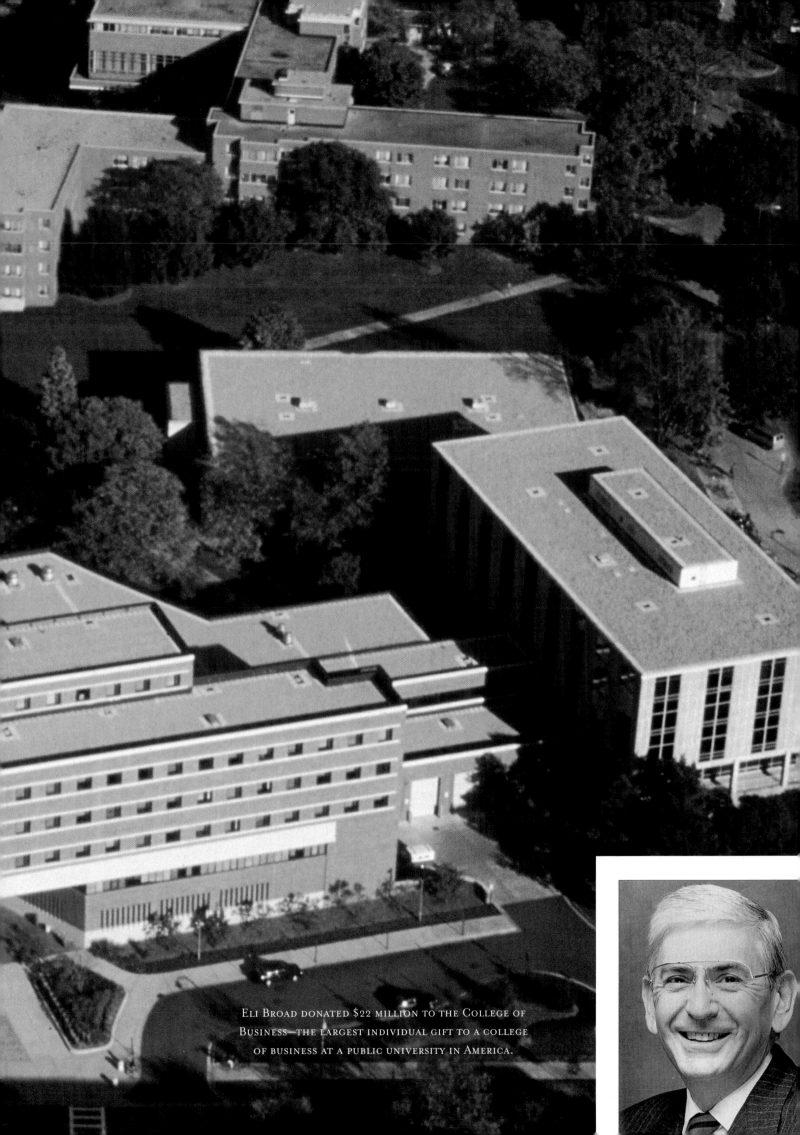

Eli Broad donated $22 million to the College of Business—the largest individual gift to a college of business at a public university in America.

College of Education

Wharton Center for Performing Arts

WHARTON CENTER FOR PERFORMING ARTS OPENED IN 1982 AND WAS NAMED FOR FORMER
UNIVERSITY PRESIDENT CLIFTON WHARTON AND HIS WIFE DOLORES WHARTON. THE CENTER HOUSES TWO THEATERS.
THE GREAT HALL SEATS 2,500; THE FESTIVAL STAGE IS MORE INTIMATE, SEATING SIX HUNDRED.
TOP PERFORMERS FROM BROADWAY AND AROUND THE WORLD HAVE GRACED THIS STAGE.

(OVERLEAF) ANOTHER VIEW OF WHARTON CENTER FOR PERFORMING ARTS.

College of Communication Arts and Science Building

Completed in 1981 at a cost of $21.5 million, the 240,000-square-foot building includes five stories of classrooms, offices and radio/television research studios. Along with the School of Journalism, the building is home to renowned WKAR television, a PBS affiliate and FM radio station. Radio began broadcasting in 1948. Television went on the air in 1954. The college was one of the first of its kind in the U.S.

Veterinary Medicine Center

A recent $46.8 million construction and renovation project now provides state-of-the-art technology and facilities for teaching and service.

College of Engineering

Anthony Hall

ANTHONY HALL AFTER ITS 1997 RENOVATION.

DETROIT COLLEGE OF LAW AT MICHIGAN STATE UNIVERSITY

The MSU Cyclotron

The premier facility of this type in North America.
On site are two superconducting cyclotrons—the K-500 and the K-1200,
the highest energy-continuous beam-accelerator in the world.

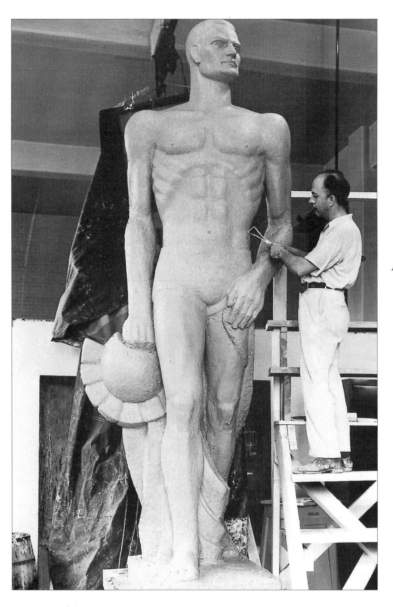

THE SPARTAN STATUE

DEDICATED ON JUNE 9, 1945.
DESIGNED BY LEONARD D. JUNGWIRTH OF MSC'S
ART DEPARTMENT, "SPARTY" STANDS TEN FEET, SIX INCHES
AND WEIGHS THREE TONS. HE IS ONE OF THE LARGEST
FREE-STANDING CERAMIC FIGURES IN THE WORLD.
IN 1925, GEORGE ALDERTON, SPORTS EDITOR FOR THE
STATE JOURNAL, PICKED THE NAME FROM A
CAMPUS CONTEST. UNFORTUNATELY, THE NAME OF THE
STUDENT WHO SUBMITTED THE ENTRY WAS LOST,
BUT THE NAME "SPARTANS" WILL LIVE FOREVER.

PRESIDENT JOHN HANNAH
PERFORMS THE UNVEILING.

JOHN SPIRIT—"SPARTY ON!"

Spartan Stadium

The twentieth-largest college-owned structure of its kind in the nation and fifth-largest in the Big Ten. Seating capacity: 72,027.

BIGGIE MUNN

BIGGIE MUNN COACHED THE SPARTANS
FROM 1947 TO 1953. HIS RECORD OF
54-9-2 MAKES HIM THE MOST
SUCCESSFUL MSU FOOTBALL COACH
OF ALL TIME. THE 1952 TEAM WENT
9-0 AND WON THE NATIONAL CHAMPI-
ONSHIP. THE 1954 TEAM WON
THE ROSE BOWL. MUNN WENT ON TO
SERVE AS THE SPARTANS' DIRECTOR
OF ATHLETICS FOR EIGHTEEN YEARS.

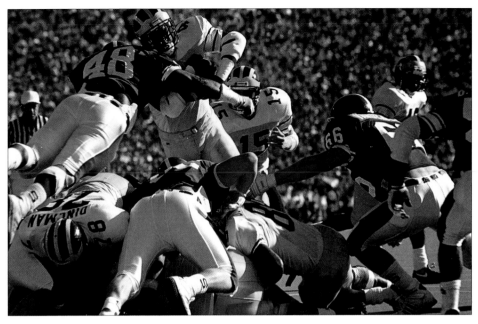

HUGH DUFFY DAUGHERTY

FOOTBALL COACH FOR NINETEEN
SEASONS. RECORD: 109-69-5.
DAUGHERTY WON TWO
BIG TEN CHAMPIONSHIPS AND ONE
NATIONAL CHAMPIONSHIP IN 1965.

MOTION

THE MSU DANCE TEAM IS A REGISTERED CLUB WITH THE MICHIGAN STATE
INTRAMURAL SPORTS AND RECREATIONAL SERVICES. MORE THAN ONE HUNDRED WOMEN TRY OUT EACH YEAR.

DUFFY DAUGHERTY FOOTBALL BUILDING

INDOOR TURF ARENA AND WEIGHT ROOM.

NICK SABAN

BECAME HEAD FOOTBALL COACH IN 1995.

(TOP) ALL AMERICAN LORENZO WHITE

(BOTOM LEFT) TWO-SPORT GREAT KIRK GIBSON

Game Day

The Clara Bell Smith
Student Athlete Academic Center

Steve Smith, Spartan, All-American basketball player, donated $2.5 million and named the building to honor the memory of his mother.

Indoor Tennis Facility

The new outdoor courts.

BAND PRACTICE BEGINS...

...GAME DAY ARRIVES

MARCHING BAND DIRECTOR JOHN MADDEN.

Homecoming Parade

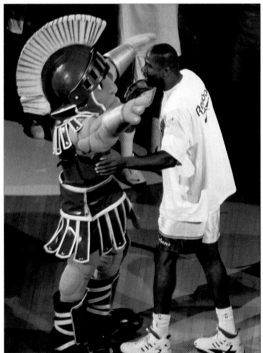

Sparty meets Magic.

JENISON
FIELDHOUSE

NAMED FOR FREDERICK C.
JENISON, A FORMER MAC
STUDENT WHO LOVED ATHLETICS
SO MUCH HE CAME TO THE
FOOTBALL FIELD EVERY DAY
TO WATCH PRACTICE.
HE BEQUEATHED MSC
A $500,000 ESTATE
TO BUILD A FIELDHOUSE.

JUD HEATHCOTE WON 340 GAMES,
LOST 220 IN NINETEEN YEARS AS THE
SPARTAN HEAD BASKETBALL COACH.
HEATHCOTE TOOK MSU TO NINE NCAA
TOURNAMENTS, WINNING THE NATIONAL
CHAMPIONSHIP IN 1979.

JENISON FIELDHOUSE TODAY IS HOME TO THE SPARTANS'
NATIONALLY RENOWNED WOMEN'S VOLLEYBALL TEAM.

(LEFT, TOP) MSU SPARTAN CHEERLEADERS

(LEFT, BOTTOM) THE LAST SHOT IN THE LAST
REGULAR SEASON GAME PLAYED IN JENISON,
MARCH 11, 1989. THE SCORE: MSU 70,
WISCONSIN 61. THE SPARTANS PLAYED AGAIN
AT JENISON IN THE SECOND ROUND OF THE NIT,
DEFEATING WICHITA STATE 79–67.

THE JACK BRESLIN STUDENT EVENTS CENTER

THE CENTER SEATS 15,100 FOR BASKETBALL.

JACK BRESLIN WAS A THREE-SPORT STANDOUT
AT MSU—FOOTBALL, BASKETBALL, AND BASEBALL.
HE WAS FOOTBALL MVP IN 1944, TEAM CAPTAIN IN 1945,
AND WENT ON TO SERVE MSU IN ADMINISTRATIVE
CAPACITIES FOR MORE THAN THIRTY YEARS. HE BECAME
KNOWN AROUND THE COUNTRY AS "MR. MSU."

TOM IZZO BECAME THE SPARTANS'
HEAD COACH IN 1995 AFTER BEING AN ASSISTANT
AT MSU FOR TWELVE YEARS.

Dorms at MSU

The largest on-campus system in the United States, with a capacity to house 17,000 students.
MSU serves 65,000 meals a day—more than any non-military institution in the world.

(OVERLEAF)

THE KELLOGG CENTER

W. K. KELLOGG, OF BREAKFAST-CEREAL FAME, ENDOWED THE KELLOGG FOUNDATION,
WHICH GAVE THE CENTER AS A GIFT TO MSU IN 1953. IT IS THE LARGEST LABORATORY IN
THE COUNTRY FOR HOTEL, RESTAURANT, AND INSTITUTIONAL MANAGEMENT. NEARLY
400,000 GUESTS ATTEND MORE THAN 1,400 CONFERENCES AND MEETINGS WITHIN THE
CENTER. IT IS ALSO HOME OF ALUMNI ASSOCIATION'S LIFELONG EDUCATION PROGRAMS.

Munn Ice Arena named for longtime MSU Football Coach and Athletic Director Clarence L. "Biggie" Munn. The Ice Arena seats 6,170 and is home ice for the national power Spartan Hockey team.

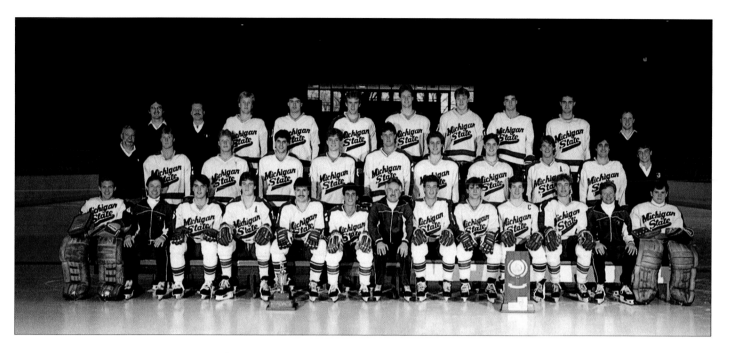

HOCKEY NATIONAL CHAMPS, 1986

RON MASON—THE COACH WITH THE MOST WINS IN THE
HISTORY OF COLLEGE HOCKEY. MASON CAME TO MSU IN
1979 AND WON THE NATIONAL CHAMPIONSHIP IN 1986.
MICHIGAN STATE ALSO WON THE NATIONAL CHAMPIONSHIP
IN 1966 UNDER HEAD COACH AMO BESSONE.

BERKEY HALL

Student Services constructed in 1957—home to Student
Government, Student Publications,
Placement Services, and other departments related to student affairs.

PLANT AND SOIL SCIENCE BUILDING

A $30 MILLION FACILITY.

The Gardens

Winter comes to campus

Spring returns!

THE RED CEDAR YACHT CLUB

A SENIOR-CLASS GIFT.

Forest Akers Golf Course, East and West

THE NEW AG PAVILLION

A STATE-OF-THE-ART FACILITY.

KRESGE ART CENTER

FOUNDED IN 1959, IT HOUSES MSU'S PERMANENT COLLECTION OF MORE THAN 4,000 WORKS OF ART
COVERING 5,000 YEARS OF HISTORY. KRESGE IS THE ONLY ART HISTORICAL MUSEUM IN CENTRAL
MICHIGAN. INCLUDED ARE SPECIAL EXHIBITIONS, STUDY AREAS, STUDIOS, CLASSROOMS, AND OFFICES.

Turfgrass Laboratory

MSU CAME UP WITH A REVOLUTIONARY METHOD
TO PUT NATURAL GRASS IN THE PONTIAC SILVERDOME
FOR THE 1994 WORLD CUP SOCCER GAMES.

Farms of MSU

MSU MEDICAL SCHOOL AND CLINICAL CENTER

HOME TO THE UNIVERSITY'S COLLEGE OF HUMAN MEDICINE, THE COLLEGE OF
OSTEOPATHIC MEDICINE, AND ITS RENOWNED FAMILY CARE PROGRAM. SINCE 1985
MSU HAS BEEN A LEADER IN MAGNETIC RESONANCE IMAGING (MRI). AS OF 1998,
MORE THAN 75,000 SCANS HAVE BEEN PRODUCED HERE.

THE W. K. KELLOGG
BIOLOGICAL STATION

THIS BEAUTIFUL MANOR HOUSE AT GULL LAKE
NEAR BATTLE CREEK WAS THE SUMMER RESIDENCE
OF W. K. KELLOGG AND WAS DEEDED TO MICHIGAN
STATE IN 1952. IT BECAME THE FINAL COMPONENT OF
THE KELLOGG GULL LAKE BIOLOGICAL STATION FOR
RESEARCH AND TEACHING. BUILT ON "EAGLE
HEIGHTS" IN 1927, THE BIRD SANCTUARY AND FARM
WERE ALSO DEEDED TO MSC IN 1928 AND 1930,
FOLLOWED BY THE KELLOGG EXPERIMENTAL FOREST
IN 1931. A $10 MILLION GRANT FROM THE
KELLOGG FOUNDATION IN 1981 PROVIDED THE
FUNDS TO RENOVATE THE PROPERTY, ADDING A NEW
ACADEMIC BUILDING, DORMITORY, CONFERENCE
FACILITIES, AND DAIRY CENTER, WHICH INCLUDED
W. K. KELLOGG'S ORIGINAL GUERNSEY HEARD.

HIDDEN LAKE GARDENS, TIPTON, MICHIGAN

MR. AND MRS. HARRY A. FEE GAVE THESE 755 ROLLING ACRES IN
SOUTHEASTERN MICHIGAN TO MSU IN 1945—FOR THE PURPOSE OF CREATING LANDSCAPE
PICTURES AND EXHIBITING AND STUDYING VALUABLE PLANT COLLECTIONS.

Spartan Stadium has many uses.

Sparty and friend.

MICK JAGGER AND THE ROLLING STONES
IN CONCERT AT SPARTAN STADIUM.

President Bill Clinton speaks at graduation.

MSU Shadows:
The Alma Mater

MSU, we love thy shadows
When twilight silence falls,
Flushing deep and softly paling
O'er ivy covered halls;
Beneath the pines we'll gather
To give our faith so true,
Sing our love for Alma Mater
And thy praises, MSU.

When from these scenes we wander
And twilight shadows fade,
Our mem'ry still will linger
Where light and shadows played;
In the evening oft we'll gather
And pledge our faith anew,
Sing our love for Alma Mater
And thy praises, MSU.

BUILDING INDEX

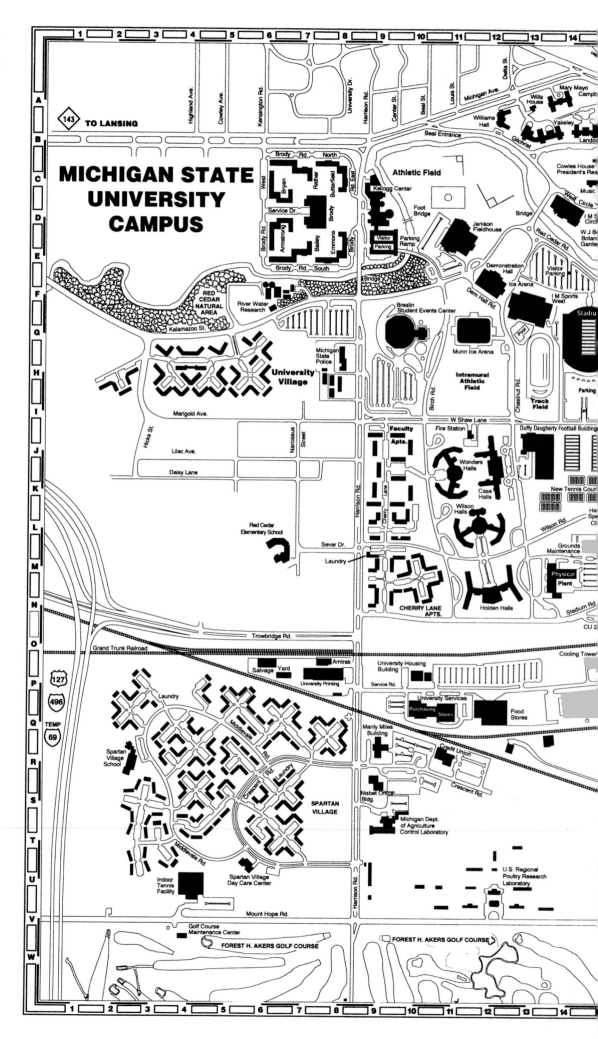

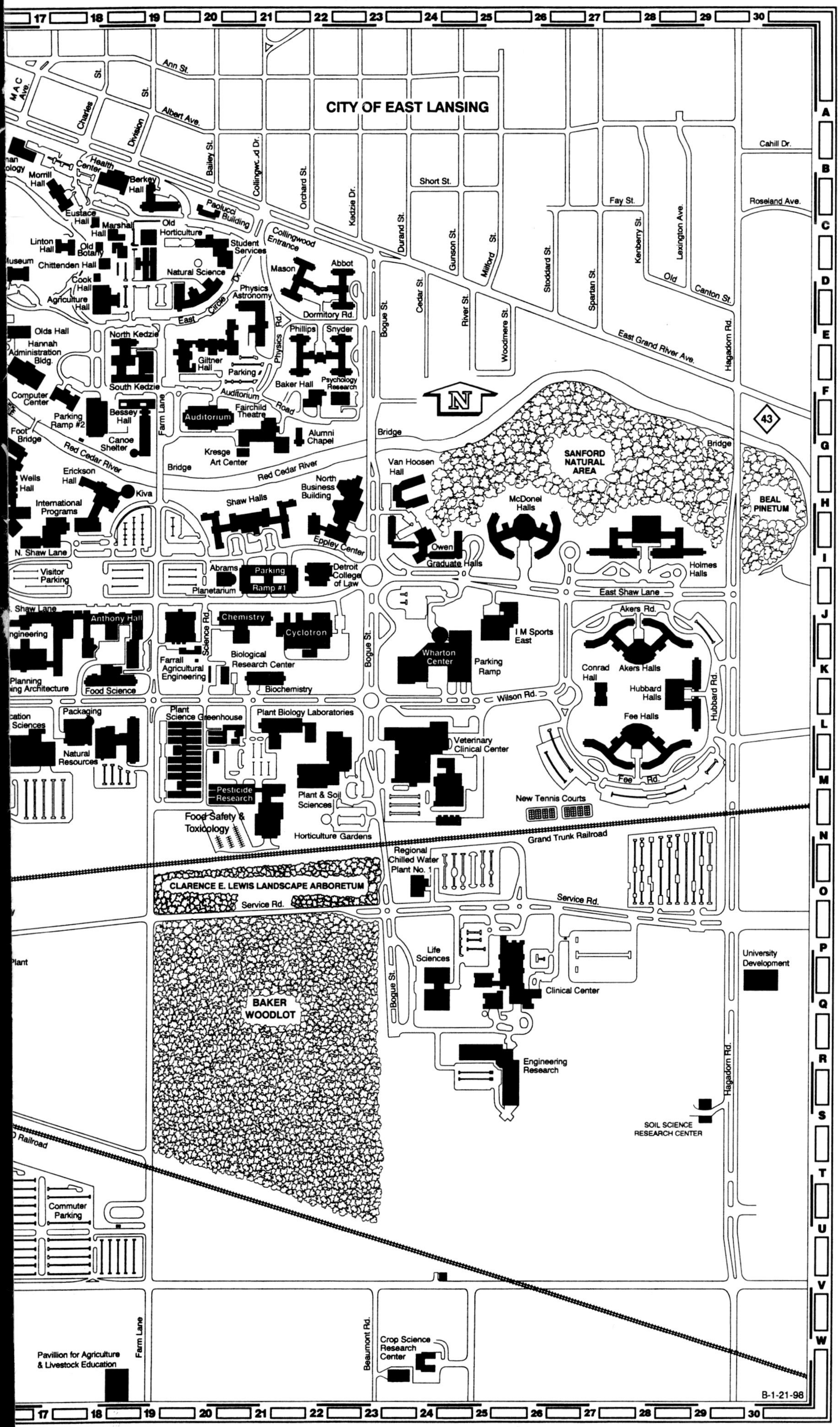

CITY OF EAST LANSING

Map labels:

MAC Ave., Ann St., Albert Ave., Charles St., Division St., Bailey St., Collingwood Dr., Orchard St., Kedzie Dr., Short St., Durand St., Fay St., Kenberry St., Roseland Ave., Cahill Dr.

Health Center, Morrill Hall, Berkey Hall, Eustace Hall, Marshall Hall, Old Horticulture, Student Services, Paolucci Building, Collingwood Entrance, Abbot, Linton Hall, Old Botany, Chittenden Hall, Natural Science, Mason, Museum, Cook Hall, Physics Astronomy, Agriculture Hall, East Circle Dr., Dormitory Rd., Olds Hall, North Kedzie, Hannah Administration Bldg., Phillips, Snyder, Computer Center, Giltner Hall, Parking, Baker Hall, Psychology Research, Parking Ramp #2, South Kedzie, Bessey Hall, Foot Bridge, Canoe Shelter, Auditorium, Fairchild Theatre, Alumni Chapel, Kresge Art Center, Red Cedar River, Wells Hall, Erickson Hall, Kiva, Bridge, Shaw Halls, North Business Building, Van Hoosen Hall, McDonel Halls, Holmes Halls, International Programs, N. Shaw Lane, Eppley Center, Owen Graduate Halls, Visitor Parking, Abrams Planetarium, Parking Ramp #1, Detroit College of Law, East Shaw Lane, N. Shaw Lane, Engineering, Anthony Hall, Chemistry, Cyclotron, I M Sports East, Akers Rd., Planning Architecture, Farrall Agricultural Engineering, Biological Research Center, Wharton Center, Parking Ramp, Conrad Hall, Akers Halls, Food Science, Biochemistry, Hubbard Halls, Education Sciences, Packaging, Plant Science Greenhouse, Plant Biology Laboratories, Wilson Rd., Fee Halls, Natural Resources, Pesticide Research, Veterinary Clinical Center, Plant & Soil Sciences, Fee Rd., Food Safety & Toxicology, New Tennis Courts, Horticulture Gardens, Grand Trunk Railroad, Hubbard Rd., Regional Chilled Water Plant No. 1, CLARENCE E. LEWIS LANDSCAPE ARBORETUM, Service Rd., Life Sciences, University Development, BAKER WOODLOT, Bogue St., Clinical Center, Engineering Research, SOIL SCIENCE RESEARCH CENTER, Commuter Parking, Farm Lane, Beaumont Rd., Crop Science Research Center, Pavilion for Agriculture & Livestock Education, Hagadorn Rd.

SANFORD NATURAL AREA, BEAL PINETUM

East Grand River Ave., Spartan St., Stoddard St., Woodmere St., Milford St., River St., Gunson St., Cedar St., Bogue St., Physics Rd., Farm Lane, Science Rd., Wilson Rd., Old Canton St., Laxington Ave.

N

43

B-1-21-98

LAUREN BROWN

Cross Country All-American, 1928.
Became track coach in 1935. Brown wore this
outfit to football games before we had Sparty.

ACKNOWLEDGMENTS

Thank you. Without your help and caring assistance this work would have been impossible. We did it the Spartan way.

Lois Bielat	Editorial Corrections
Bev VandenBerg	Assistant
Paulette Martis	Sports Information
Fred L. Honhart	Archives
Debbie Hettinger	Secretary
Freida Martin	IMC
Jack Wolf	Hidden Lake Gardens
Scott Breckner	The Breslin Center
Laura Progyn	W. K. Kellogg Biological Station
ABC Sports	
Bob Brent	Artist
Ken Horvath	Golf Coach
Gene Orlando	Men's Tennis Coach
Larry Sierra	Director of Intramurals and Recreation Services
Kim Hopkins	MSU Printshop
Kurt Dewhurst	Museum

Contributing Photographers

Ruth Tanner	Photographer
Peter DeLong	Alumnus
Bruce Fox	MSU Media Relations
Kevin W. Fowler	Sports Information
Tony Rogalski	Professional Photographer
John Penrod	Penrod/Hiawatha
Kim Hopkins	Photographer
Nicole Ohl	Photographer
Roger Boettcher	Photographer
Larry Bielat	Amateur Photographer
Steve Deming	Photographer
Winebrenner	Photographer

To order or for information contact:
Scott Bielat
ASAP Inc.
P.O. Box 25
Novi, MI 48374
(248) 374-0021

Michigan State has won a number of National Championships other than football, basketball, and hockey:
Men's Cross Country: 1939, 1948, 1958, 1959
Men's Wrestling: 1967 (*Coach Grady Peninger*)
Men's Soccer: 1967, 1968 (*Coach Gene Kenny*)
Men's Gymnastics: 1958 (*Coach George Szypula*)